THE
RUSH
OF LAVA
FLOWERS

LYDIA POPOWICH

This book is dedicated to my friends Jeanette Scull and Geoff Weston

Blood, sex, magic and loss punctuate this collection of powerful poems tracing a life shaped by hereditary trauma. History is found not only in books but in our bones and in our dreams. The Rush of Lava Flowers celebrates the strength of human spirit for like the plants that grow back on the edge of a volcano after an eruption people are endlessly resilient. Hope never dies. These poems speak not just of one life but of our times as the trauma of war and migration continues to haunt future generations. The confessional poems with a surrealist twist are written in a diverse range of styles and will sweep you away on an emotional journey across unexpected landscapes.

"I found this collection scorchingly beautiful. There is a glittering darkness. A deep cut of a journey. Wonderful."
Martyn Hesford, poet and screenwriter.

"These vibrant, lively poems constitute the chronicle of a journey through life. The language throughout is clear, with a jazzy cello-like music, open to surprise and disappointment and the tragedy of history as well as the joy and agony of living. Lydia Popowich's poems pull you into a world of images and archetypes, where everything at first glance seems at odds with everything else but then, word by word, poem by poem, the poet's skill allows her unique voice to guide you through the reality of the emotional and the material world. Lydia Popowich does what all poets do, which is to write the lyrics of survival and hope that humanity needs, putting beauty back into the broken shards of our age and she does so with a rare and genuine selfless honesty. She pulls the world through the eye of her needle. Anyone interested in contemporary poetry should read this book."
George Gunn, poet and playwright.

CONTENTS

RUPTURE

PROLOGUE

a strange dawn uncurls
oyster pink I am breathing
alone in my shell

ZERO TO TEN

In the beginning, I count down cigarettes and orange
scorched days in the dark cocoon of Now, Voyager.
I devour red velvet and the upsurge of your heartbeat.

In my first year you are out of reach on the marble
shelf as I ride my silver cross carriage to the Castle.
I want a warm drink not clocks and candle sticks.

In my second year my meandering footprints are cast
in cement and the violence of passing trains.
I feel the sting of Aztec girls and foreign tongues.

In the missing year I watch electric light triangulate
as my door is wedged open by the white coats.
Beyond glass, snow falls and you wave from a distance.

In my fourth year you lug my dead weight to pointless
rotations of my left foot. *Good girl,* says the physio.
My reward is crumbling bread for ducks in Lister Park.

In my fifth year Miss Blowers raps me over the head
with Noddy and the Magic Rubber. *Stop talking,* she says.
I wet my pants. Why are scissors always too blunt?

In the sixth year, semolina congeals but my lips are sealed.
Red-faced, father dances a vodka jig by the camp fire.
Rubbing my knees, I am told nettle stings are good for you.

In my seventh year, I hide within canoodles of trees
by the Leeds and Liverpool, stay silent when you scream
my name. Rain beads sycamore leaves like mercury.

In my eighth year, I survey the crater of an extinct volcano,
see you small and alone down below. Turning circles,
you shout my name. I hear the rush of lava flowers.

In the nothing year, I leave myself behind in a waiting room.
The quick brown fox jumps over the lazy dog. Parallel bars
and surgical scars. I watch as chrysanthemums sour in vases.

In my tenth year, legs braced for action I'm back to school.
They say they've missed my piano playing and mysterious
chalk drawings. I carve a car from balsa wood. My knife slips.

ARTERIO VENOUS

Her country was besieged.
The Great Saphenous Vein,
a lonesome road to nowhere,
a waste-land, booby-trapped with incendiaries.
Scarpa's Triangle sailed a quiet sea
and Hunter's Canal lay stagnant.

Beyond a cotton screen of chrysanthemums
her body bore a map no longer secret,
sketched out in biro, red for arteries, blue for veins.
Red and blue make purple, she'd learned at school.
Legs splayed a landscape across the table,
roads and rivers marked
soft, pale flesh, inert on padded leather.
Like seagulls scavenging an empty shore
the white coats gathered in freezing stares
while she traced the tangle of petals,
leaves and stems interwoven beyond.

Pointless, she listened to foreign tales;
remembered a white horse
galloping circles in the wind,
her purple coat flapping open
as she ran down the road.

LEEDS 76

The ambulance man with striking
green eyes stroked the inside
skin of her teenage arm as she lay
strapped (for her own safety)
on the reeking canvas of another NHS.
If you're a lucky girl you'll meet Jimmy!

She thought he was, maybe
trying to be nice (but those alien
fingers were electric…) No comfort
blanket, suspended in L10 skeletal
traction, legs akimbo, a monster
from a fairy tale. The male
nurse with watery grey eyes brought gin
secrets in a Barr's Cream Soda bottle, hot
take-away through her open window
of gritty nights. She thought he was, maybe,
trying to be nice (but gin made her sick).

The glass half-full on the sunny side.
Cheer up, might never happen,
said the porter with lizard pink
eyes taking her down to a strip
-lit basement, down corridors
lined with conduits.
If you're a lucky girl you'll meet Jimmy!

THE DOCTOR ALWAYS RINGS TWICE

Afterwards, mama offered
tea in bone china
spiked with roses, edged with gold.

The sugar tongs we never used
lay centre stage on the lace tablecloth.
His fingers struggled with the dainty cup.

Mama looked away when a stain
bled across the virgin white.
In the next room, I smoothed down

the pleats of my school uniform,
pulling up my socks
as far as they would go.

THE MISSING

One by one they pass blind
through the living arch,
the children of loss following
Mother's twisted path of breadcrumbs.
Blue birds peck at their bare feet.
The sun bubbles over yellow fields
where cats sleep away the shadows
of the deep purple wood.

One by one they stray,
broken children with tender skin;
tawny robin's wing, freckled amber,
cuckoo spit, sun kissed pebble, raven's
feather, morning mist and midnight pools,
following Mother's cinder path
through the crystal orchard where apples
hang, red and flawless but out of reach.

One by one they stumble, feet bleeding
on Mother's razor path of barbs
into the dark. Snakes circle, whisper
warning but the children do not hear.
Their fingers seek between the snapping
branches but find no-one. Their tears
blossom roses no-one will ever see
in the depths of the purple wood.

The hermit snips and sews silence
in her cave in the deep purple wood.
She threads her needle with the fine hair
of a nameless girl, makes painstaking
stitches, a cloak of perfect skin; tawny
robin's wing, freckled amber, cuckoo spit,
sun-kissed pebble, raven's feather,
morning mist and midnight pools.

PARTITION

Beyond glass the gypsy girl
is flying a kite, a red spiral
in a forget-me-not sky.

In the next field a tractor
scars the earth dispersing
a cloud of fine brown dust.

Then, from nowhere
the snow comes, blinding,
vertiginous, unnatural

in May. Luminous pearls
erase my shadows, filling
the cracks in the corners

of my small room. Colours
pale to surrender, baby
powder, eggshell and bone.

Precipitation; an ice flow.
The glacial bed calves
a table, a chair. My limbs

crystallise. Beyond glass
the sun dazzles, the gypsy
girl has vanished and you

shelter in the sharpness
of rhododendrons not
in bloom. You are waving,

you are waving - smiling
but I am your snow child
and I can't wave back.

The Magic Mirror

I am the eye in the wall, unblinking
as you twist in your dreams.

I am mistress of deceit calling you,
naming you, mornings and evenings.

I am silver and pure delight
of thin brittle skin slithering

over your shame. Like winter
I bite envy into your bones.

Mermaids swoon in my whirlpools.
Beetles and lizards creep, frogs doze

in my tangled borderlands.
White lilies fade to bronze beneath

your selfie gaze. My heart
is a diamond you will never find.

You so want to break me
but you will only break yourself.

THE DARKENING

Shadows rooted in the sour
grooves that framed
her mouth. Invisible at first,
they bloomed in the living
map of her face, festered
in the lines on her brow,
in the web of crow's feet
perched on cheekbones
and in every pore
of once perfect skin.
Within purple moons
beneath shuttered eyes
darkness multiplied
spread along the wrinkles
of her neck, the valley
between breasts, the soft
folds of belly and genitals,
filling hollows and dimples
down to the pink tips
of her toes. Eventually
shadows enveloped her
like a miasmic cloak.
In the mirror she saw
memories of memories
and not the shudder
of dust she had become.
In the street, folk saw
a swirl of fog and not
a woman. They walked
through her and shivered.
Her words became a wild
keening of wind, creatures
of night her only friends.
Bats, moths, owls gathered
safe in her twilight wake.

THE BORROWERS

We drift in the wind, elusive, mercurial
as scraps of tinsel. We hunt human
gatherings, crossing forests, seas
and cities. Passing from home to home,
we reap your memories, your secrets
that doze like fish in a torpid pool.
You mistake us for sunbeams,
for insects in the sultry night, for snow
-flakes on your child's face or candle
light soft in your lover's eyes. Like air
we enter your nasal passages, seeping

into your skin and every private cavity.
We grub deep into the coils of grey
where you hide. Without you, we are empty
as a church without the presence of God.
We can't love, we can't hate, we can't sing.
So when you reach the top of the stairs
and forget why you are there, when you fail
to recall your mother's voice or the taste
of beer, when you forget the meal you ate
ten minutes before and your own name,
please don't mind too much.

GRAVEL ROADS

There was fire over water the night
we met, sparks aplenty. You were more
elegant than expected, curvaceous steel

with a hint of rebellion. Your body
enclosed me like a rocket on our way
to a mysterious planet. My heartbeat

quickened as I fondled the unfamiliar
instruments swathed in your green light.
Together we claimed space, unstoppable.

We shot across the Tyne Bridge without
looking back, headed north, crossing
borders and north – north – anticipating

the friction of car wheels on gravel
roads. There were torn rainbows, strings
of pearls, demons hiding in hedgerows,

lightning bolts and blinding spider mist.
There were herring seas, twisted forests,
and languid nights of Summer Isles. Lost

in the clouds we met only talking cats.
Fairy lights beckoned from peat bogs;
temptation lurking in each red window.

We were Bonny and Clyde, a foxy
duo kicking up shit in the badlands until
we broke with a whimper not a bang.

I feel the cold without you and doubt
the presence of soul. Scars fade in sun;
nothing remains but moss, rust and bone.

On Visiting John o'Groats

It can take most of your life to see
the large car park at the end of the line.
There are no instructions on arrival.
You circulate widdershins and search

the large car park at the end of the line
for a space that suits your personality.
You circulate widdershins and search
a familiar face in the day-glow crowds

for a space that suits your personality.
Some of them are smiling and holding
a familiar face in the day-glow crowds.
How many coffee beans in the jar?

Some of them are smiling and holding
hands. It's important to guess
how many coffee beans in the jar.
Green sunglasses are optional, reflective

hands. It's important to guess
how many miles to Land's End?
Green sunglasses are optional, reflective
blisters on the soles of your feet.

How many miles to Land's End?
You might travel naked and grateful for
blisters on the soles of your feet.
It can take most of your life to see.

PLOT AND BASH

Tackle it when thrust through the window.
Look difficult when leaving the control area,
keeping right. Drive gentle up the road.
There may be more than you.
It will contain the time and distance you.
Get to the first junction as somebody else
and set off again. Beware of blindly following.
He may know where he is going or he may not.
Keep trying to make the fit and keep an eye on.
You may end up lost off route, being baffled
on route! Alternative. Pull up, obstruct and try
the hand better than clutter. With practise
you will plot the move keeping at least two.
If you are baffled it may be your opinion
-miracles do happen and he may see. Do it
or provide the clue. As a last resort guess.
Don't stumble on a code. Use a magnifier.
Don't discard handouts, keep them safe.
Engineer the maps in alphabetical
to easily locate you in the night.

IT'S BETTER TO KNOW

this is not a love
poem, the howl of storm

pain, the rain inside.
The forever house

on the dead end lane,
over-grown, deeply

rutted tracks, bordered
by forget-me-nots.

Two plain Janes stand
guard with crucifixes

and bibles of grief.
They point to the sky,

dispense sunglasses.
Is everything fair

in love or war?
It's better to know.

Go open the door,
look into the dark.

INNER SPACE

Dreaming of grass in crisis, I search.
I make the first cut, split the almost sphere.
Fear hides under the floor like worms
whispering small acts of sabotage, close,
close as skin. Secret notes, names scribbled

on scraps. Deep in pools of contagion,
each transparent history will keep repeating
subsonic booms. I am watching you dance
in the rain, stirring the surface calm
into chaotic patterns. I see you at the end

taking hold the awe. It is beautiful
to quietly slip under in this bog country.
Northerlies and the listless spin the wonder.
The river carves a silver snake under septic
skies while the moon hangs by a thread.

ˋ

Postcards from Utopia

February
They say the first time is the hardest,
stepping out of your skin like an old car.
You cling to the broken parts, the frayed.

March
At dawn, camellias rain from a veiled sky.
We walk barefoot and sing as we work.
There is no fear of falling. You must come.

April
A special day- my renaming. I am now Sister
Calpurnia, a cup to be filled. At last I am
connected, unashamed. They drink my nectar.

May
There is symmetry and straight lines, green
on white. The blinds are transparent. A life
less miscellaneous but binding.

June
I have stopped remembering my dreams.
Is this a problem or a blessing? I miss coffee
and books but there is no need for increase.

July
Silence from you? Are you coping? Does Sasha
entertain with his rodents? Cats are banned here.
I miss mirrors and your dirty laugh.

August
Uniformity is freedom. We move, sunbeams
across the fields. We congregate, peel away
like marigold petals. Love me, love me not.

September
Brother Gabriel was recycled today. He cried
with pride as we staked him in the cornfield.
The crows are circling as we prepare our feast.

November
Sister Evangeline reported me for deviance.
Tomorrow they will remove my canines, shave
my fur. I will begin again. Patience, my love.

LIGHTING THE BLUE TOUCH PAPER

One winter's night in Ashington, Tim went looking
for paradise and found her swinging
slowly to and fro in the play park. She was singing
an old tune from a Rodgers and Hammerstein musical.
At first he thought the canny moonlight made her blue
or a street lamp malfunction. On closer scrutiny

he was blown away by her truth; her hair of delphinium,
her eyes of forget-me not, her lips of cyanide,
her skin of palest sky, her fingers of summer solstice,
her kingfisher boots and hyacinth thighs. He forgot his need
to score and mounted the roundabout, sort of casual, like.
In a nervous, squeaky voice he offered top-grade weed

but got no reply. She kicked up and swung higher,
carolling the refrain of 'Some Enchanted Evening',
laughing through teeth of gleaming steel.
So, how's 'bout coffee at mine then? he trilled.
She fell back to earth and followed him home.
Her name was Geraldine.

When dawn broke he woke to her singing
'Oh What a Beautiful Morning' as she made breakfast.
In the bright light she was cornflower
and so was the scrambled egg, cornflakes and toast.
My touch turns the whole world blue, she said.
Looking down at his naked torso, he was amazed.

So, Tim changed the colour of his spots,
redecorated the flat, ditched drugs and shop-lifting.
He married Geraldine. Together they opened up
Blue Mood Foods, a take-away near the Crematorium.
They had two kids, Odin and Astrid
in subtle shades of ocean. Then the letters began;

complaints about the changing hue of the town,
concerns about Health and Safety, the loss of grey.
They were served a court order forcing Geraldine
to wear gloves in public places. There was a petition
demanding her repatriation to wherever. One blue moon
she vanished with the kids and without leaving a note.

Tim moved to Hull and got a job slaughtering pigs.
He took pride in his work, keeping the stun gun
by his bed, next to the blueprint family photo.

THE A TO Z OF THE APOCALYPSE

Atrocity is a wall of thorns artless
Bluebottles smashing against glass fall
Comatose to my window ledge making
Death their next great adventure
Escape to shit scented nirvanas
Filled with lost winged kin and divine
Garbage heaps piss-fountains free from
Human malevolence effervescent
Incandescence and decay so promising
Jesus died without seeing
Knowledge is an act of sabotage not
Limitless power but a weapon
Mother warned me about the elitist
Noah and his treachery for not
One soul is more holy than another
Paradise is an orange wasteland where
Quicksand and alligators devour
Revolutionaries with their fiery
Socks and fondness for the insignificant
Turtle neck sweaters may be aesthetically
Unpleasing but they conceal the frogs in
Virtuous throats raising the alarm on
Wet Wednesdays when there are no boats
Xpected but gin is being served at Erith
Yacht club as waves lap and lightening
Zaps the three wise monkeys at the door.

ROCK

THE GLEANING

I follow Mama's crooked
path beyond the giant privet hedge

where once I found blackbird eggs. Perfect
spheres of eau de nil slipped through careless

fingers and smashed on paving stones set by Papa
years before. The shed cowers beneath the apple tree

where once I found God. Perched up top, he was singing
Bowie songs and watching the neighbours through binoculars.

Ashes to ashes; Jennifer Jones kissed the coal man.
Dust to dust; Marjorie Moony hoovered nude.

I never done good and I never done bad.
I wanna come down right now and try

Mama's apple pie, but never
say why, never say, never say.

MORTALITY

We follow the signs, white on blue
autumn clouds shifting. Slings
and arrows show one way to exit.
We follow the twisted pitted road
down the line. We avoid potholes,
broken tarmac, pines felled by storms
littering the verge. We drive slowly
around those tight bends. The road
south unspools an old home movie.
In Golspie the doors burst open,
the sun breaks gilding the moss,
the dry stone walls, the sycamores.
The paramedic with kind eyes
wishes you breath. Magic
moss crumbles gold dust
between your fingers until
only the scent of earth remains.

THE RUNNER

rose from the sea at dawn as sun
funnelled across Burrigill Bay.

    Her long black hair trailed a seine net
slack from her fisherman's cap.

    In the shadows of the stacks
she bore down on the eastern shore

    casting off wrack and bilge water.
Her feet, bloodless as starfish, spiked the shingle.

    The life of the sea spilled
from her oilskins. She ran dead

    ahead up the hill through meadows
glazed with dew and sheep,

    passing the busted creel boat
aslant and hulled with bog myrtle.

    Clouds frothed on the horizon
in a herringbone breeze as she ran

    to the crest
where an old hen waited by the gate

                    and one wall of a ruined croft pointed
             skywards like a prayer.

THE WOUNDED

There was nothing but the hunt,
the pain, the struggle, the dark.
She had to keep running. Run!
She could barely recall a time
before the breaking of branches.
She could barely recall her time
of being human, of skin
touching skin and naked picnics
when she gazed boldly at the sun.
In her upright days moss and wild
flowers sprang from her every
footstep, birds sang her every word.

Now she ran on all fours. Run, run!
Her cloven hooves were raw, spiked
by thorns. She was pierced by nine
arrows, fur rank with pus. Venomous.
Calculating. The forest was silent,
a lifeless zodiac of roots and branches.
She could no longer recall her name
or why she had to run. Her lungs failed
and she fell in the shadow of a crippled
tree. As she waited for her joyful exit,
forked lightning unravelled silver
threads of hope across the night sky.

December Storm

We drive south into a ferrous wind,
the sky unclenching. Fingers of rust
stain the peaks of Morven and Scaraben,
old blood on a crumpled sheet.
The land trembles with yesterday's news

barbed and shredded. Bales of hay sheathed
in pink stack the sweetness of last summer.
Sheep dot and dash the fields like broken
teeth spat into a steel bowl. Crofts cower,
trees twist into submission. Amputation

-dislocation. Strike a pose. Resistance
is futile. Across the border smoke rises,
thin entrails signalling your departure.

YOU WERE SOMEONE ELSE

the last time   I saw you   corroded man of metal
manoeuvring   your mortal shell over tarmac   breathless
outside the travel inn   cyber sun sparked bodywork   so
blinding you didn't see   me at the window sipping irn bru
your brittle head shadowed by your panama   dipped dead
-pan you looked like a famous italian film director shooting
the scandalous biopic of an unknown nazi   my father
forged by stalin's holodomor man of steel with the ability
to change shape become uniform less liable   to crack
the annealing boy with a sword such handsome cheek-bones
they burned   villages on the western steppes belching black
smoke like answers on the day paramilitary death squads took
photographs   I dreamed of you behind the wheel of a red
volkswagen   your shameful love of german engineering
your welded lips breaking down reforming internal shapes under
pressure   like swarfiga green jelly in a tub   your giant
hand scarred by hundreds of burns   wounds carved deep
never given a chance   to heal working fourteen hour shifts
at the foundry   *get on board* you said   words stuck
in your throat when they took your rotten teeth out   you
coughed blood and lies into a white cotton handkerchief
pretended to hang yourself with a jump   freedom is a gift
not for everyman   you were someone else in 1942
metal   pushed   through   a die

THE DAY SHE DROPPED

             the trifle, it exploded on blue tiles pain
-ting cryptic signs churned in chaos.
Raspberries, cream, vanilla custard, glace cherries, perfect
sponge, (home-made of course) secrets
hinted by hundreds and thousands
no-one would ever understand. The cold
glister of broken crystal, the old bowl her ex
brought back from Paris at his own risk.
She wanted to laugh until she saw
his face at the head of the table, the half
-empty bottle of Smirnoff, his plate strewn with left-over
Christmas, the scrunched up paper napkin, handy for blood
spilt when she tried to pick up the pieces.

THE WINTER BREAK

The blizzard began, cherry blossom from a flame sky. The road home
vanished. Pink ice floes shape-shifted in the river, bumping
and grinding like clubbed seals. We tended the fire
and played strip poker. In bed you wore lipstick and a balaclava.

On the third day we tracked through the crystal forest. The valley
was a fandango of silence. I clawed at it with my bare hands
You held your phone up high, immobile as the Statue of Liberty.
We returned to the cabin and played Scrabble with four letter words.

The windows became peepholes. I saw no footprints in the virgin drift,
only the farmer's wife floating silver between the tree tops.
She was wearing a wolf jacket, her face upturned to the falling snow.
That night you thought you heard singing in the wind.

On your last day, you stopped speaking, stayed in bed, a tender huddle
of bones. I roasted meat on the log fire and drank Jack Daniels. I recited
the tale of our first New Year's Eve, kissing in Times Square
while rockets fell. I could still remember the neon taste of your flesh.

INTERSECTION, INVERNESS

Alone, I wait for the green
light at a T junction. In my rear view

mirror, mother and daughter, blonde curls, matching
smiles, laughing, chatting, trading

glances, milky eyed reflections of one
another, safe as air bubbles in fused

glass; on their way home from Asda or ballet or violin
class or fish and chips with grandma after swimming

or Maeve's birthday party and the promise of girl
guiding. The lights change, I turn

away from the crimson
city, away from the sighs of cherry blossom

in the ranked rows of trees on the riverside
as petals freeze to pink ice in the chill.

DETACHED

In 1963 we moved to a bungalow halfway up a dead
end street, a red brick box with bay windows staring;
doors painted blue and yellow, fancy stained glass
and apple trees bordering the Leeds and Liverpool.

At Sycamore Drive we played no hide and seek;
four rooms, a bath, perfect for three. I learned strange
words, detached, overtime, cul-de-sac. I learned
the conspiracy of mirrors and how to polish glass.

The parlour belonged to untouchables, Capo Di Monte
folk arranged on lace doilies, lead crystal birds perched.
So we circled in the living room, floored by checks.
Above the fire a silver mirror hung by a chain.

There, mama posed every morning to wind rollers,
powder cheeks with Yardley, fix lipstick. Father carved
jam and cheese sandwiches on the Formica table, self built,
the drawer lined with felt; forks, knives in compartments.

By the bay window, one armchair upholstered in daisies
turned an angle away from the view of wooded hillsides,
river snaking south. Back to my mama straightening
stockings, tightening her girdle while papa studied maps.

The Contest

If only Eve could don a straw hat and vanish to the Isle of Paros!
Instead, she was trapped in the Garden, weaving hard lines

of blood as the beginning people judged her pink lady tears.
Where was her power over water? Lilith dried out in the desert.

They shall possess her forever and dwell there
from generation to generation.

As the mushroom cloud rose over the maroon lagoon
Eve wondered if it was, in fact, a good time for a trip.

She was wearing her lucky pearls and the new horizon
walking boots, birthday gifts from the ferryman.

It is He who casts the lot for them,
And with His hands He marks off their shares of her.

Sad to see swine die but she was really more of a snake person.
So she turned her last page with the left hand

of darkness and prepared to recycle her perfect skin,
gala smooth and hoping for first prize. Ka-Ching!

INHERITANCE

No-one knows the people of bone
or why my drunken Dedushka brought them home
from an auction room on Lawkholme Lane,
textile wages blown on beer, cigarettes and porcelain.
Their unexpected arrival, smooth and brittle,
put Babushka in a flutter
flapping about with her feather duster
finding the best place for aristocracy.
The old king with daughter at his knee
and her lover, typecast, ensnared eternally
by some secret quandary, unaware
of their position centre stage.

On a white cherry blossom day
I sipped cider with my lover on Lawkholme Lane
while Player's No 6 sucked Dedushka away,
left Babushka alone with royalty.
No-one knows their story, how it ends.
They hover inside my door, uninvited,
the bone people atop the tall cabinet
next to the clock. I make my entrances
and exit, looking up as I pass by.

Keighley Gala

I'm seven feet high astride your shoulders bombing
through electric crowds in Victoria Park. The air

dynamites with diesel, sweat and sugar. I'm assaulted
by neon fantasy, a vertigo of blue and orange. Your hands

grip my calves, fingers laced with scars. The cloying scent
of Brylcreem like candy floss wafts from your hair.

There's a rumour of Hell's Angels, a tremor in the summer
night. Families are leaving early. I'm the only child riding

gilded ponies. You don't see me waving as you inhale
another Players. Six pence a turn at Hook a Duck, goldfish

beaming from bubbles. You hand over a shilling, wait
for change that never comes. He mutters, *bloody foreigner.*

On the long walk home I feel a dribble down my thigh.
Goldie's little mouth opens, closes and then stills.

NODDY SPEAKS IN TONGUES

Break-time. The others sip milk through a straw, crunch crisps.
I am the foreign kid, cornered by Miss Blowers, *stick the tip*
between your teeth. The them there this. The they them, like this.
Her tongue protrudes from her mouth like a sliver of salami.
De dem dare dis. De dey dem, like dis, I repeat.

Miss Blowers holds Noddy and the Magic Rubber. Her sharp
fingernails tap the cover; rat-a-tat, rat-a-tat, rat-a-tat. Thwack.
I am crowned with Noddy. I detonate with pain and shame.
The they them there this. The they them! roars Miss Blowers.
My tongue strikes, *three thunderous thumps, thanks.*

Back home Mama prepares borscht, slicing beetroots, carrots,
Chop, chop, chop into small. Her knife slides through red
flesh with no resistance, taps as it hits the chopping board.
Don't like bosh, says I. *Not de bosh, but de borscht!* says she.
*Not de borscht but **the** borscht* and out comes my tongue.

THE BLACK BROOM

Belly craves bread as big as a cloud, remembering Kiev.
Her family silver chimes, a sound that remembers Kiev.

The train is descending into the dark, she prays, eyes open
in her corner pissing with the crowd who remember Kiev.

Knives forks spoons traded for apple cores, potato peelings, crusts
of German rye bread. Not so proud, she still remembers Kiev.

Duck eggs like nuggets of sea water, a cup of pigweed soup;
her belly shrinks to a fist, a scowl which remembers Kiev.

There's no turning back, condemned *an enemy of the people.*
The black broom stole her song, she's too cowed to remember Kiev.

Belly rebels, not pigweed soup but wet dreams of strawberries
with cream and ploughed English fields. She vows to remember Kiev.

The Channel churns white cliffs, a bluebird cloud. Remember Kiev?
Belly spews her name out loud, unbowed, remembering Kiev.

HEARTLAND

I

The train is leaving but I am here
in a yellow room with curtains of sky.
The door is chained from the inside,
the lock and the mirror are broken.

The train is leaving and you're not here.
The prints of army boots have scarred
the wood I once polished on my hands
and knees with melting candle wax.

The train is leaving, I can hear it's wail.
On the sunlit balcony above treetops
where the birds have fallen silent,
a young boy hangs from a rope.

The train is leaving to I know not where
but my cat is hungry, my roses wilt,
poor Mishka waits on the window sill
and they will not fit in my suitcase.

II

Will I find you arched across wild waters?
Will I see you in the sparks of burning pines?
Will you shimmer like an island in an ocean of wheat?
Will I smell you in the northerly like the promise
of snow or grass that is limpid green?
Will I meet you in the white lines in the middle of the road
as I speed in a Stravinsky crescendo?
Will I catch you like a ghost in a speaking mirror?
Will I taste you in buttermilk pancakes
or tea sweetened with cherry jam?
Will I feel you in the blue fur of a cat?
Will I discover you folded inside yourself
like a secret at the back of my wardrobe?
Will I fear you in my dreams of showers without water
or scroll you on my screen as a drone
follows the River Dnieper Mama once swam?
Will I hear you in the trains as they scream through the night?

YEARS OF LIVING DANGEROUSLY

1933
Babushka kept a pig in the bathtub
while the Red Army raided barns
and larders enforcing Holodomor.
Out on the Kiev streets stick bodies
staggered, bloated and staining
snowdrifts like squashed blueberries.

The children named the pig Nina
against their mother's warnings.
Come slaughter day they waited
on the balcony with scarves tight
round their ears but the screams
rang loud and their tears froze.

1974
The British three day week; fish, chips
by candlelight. I strutted my hot pants
to Bowie and Bolan on Pirate Radio;
sniggered when Papa built secret shelves
inside the chimney breast to hide tins
of flour, sugar, rice, pasta and preserves.

Babushka, me and Mama chopped
and shredded cabbage, carrots, onions
like swathes of virgin lace spilling
over the yellow table, pickled in old
sweetie jars with faded labels. The blue
room soured with the stink of vinegar.

2020
The year of Covid; I empty bookcases,
arrange tins of soup, sweetcorn and tuna.
Lockdown. The silent sky tumbles
sapphires while stags browse my garden.
Their antlers spark a murder
of crows spooling from the willows.

When the amber light fades to dusk
ghosts come knocking at my door.
I look out at a deserted street, counting
down every wavering heart
beat. In the still mountain night
I hear the echo of Babushka cheering.

RAIN

YOUR POEM

The passage of one life is like a poem,
the end an echo of the start; a solitary
fight to enter this world, darkness
to light. The bloodying of white
sheets observed by strangers in a room
with thin curtains, mirrored in the final
stanza only without felicitations.
You hope you die before you get old.

The romance, the action, the clues lie
in the middle section of your poem,
an exposition on your main theme;
a search for happiness, love, money,
acceptance, fluffy cats, fame, red hair,
a good shag or prize-winning dahlias.
You hope you die before you get old.
Whatever floats your boat, baby!

By stanza seven you learn you are not
a boat but a desert island, unexplored.
You hope you die before you get old.
You sit on the shore watching the murky
tide of water and wait for the Ferry. Angel
whispers in your ear. It is the jade game,
the sky is not the same blue, the sun holds
no heat and no one will ever truly get you.

In stanza nine the diminishing begins.
Your body shrinks (except for your nose).
You shape-shift, spend more time looking
down and back. Chins multiply but hair
and friendships fall away. Downsizing.
You hope you die before you get old.
You can't piss in a pot no more.
You can't recall names no more.

You hope you die before you get old.
The passage of your life is like a poem
structured by repetition, rhythm, rhyme,
recurring motifs and metaphors exploring
a theme (same shit different day). The arc,
the meaning of your story remains hidden
to you (although strangers see) until
the moment God turns over your page.

DOWN BELOW

She has never seen so many of them, diving
in ribbons, mercurial as the heart of a virgin.
She opens her mouth to cry out, joyful
her hot mouth expects a fierce Atlantic roar.

She taps an elegant rhythm as the rocks tease.
Not surprised, they reflect the enduring
equivalence of a human. Five liquid bodies
hurl into the waves. She's eager to slip

a knot around her waist, slide into the silver
gaping mouth. She believes she will fly
underwater, melding like angler fish, one
into a luminous other. Love lingers

under the scalloped tongue and her smile
disappears into a cave. Words are the agony
of a different folly, wafer thin, hankering
for the heavenly parts of this world.

COLLISION

The day the waves came,
she went out looking.
Rocks, boats slashed by winter,
White Rose half-painted on the quay.
The beach swirled diamonds,
wind down-turning creels.
The Café closed tight,
shuddering on the line
where elements collide.
The Orkney Ice Cream sign
askew by the door, keening
like a gull with a broken wing.
In the bothy he burned
a fire of peat, warming
fingers, interwoven. He breathed
the secrets of seashells into her ear.
The sky splintered beyond the window pane,
words drowning as oceans swelled a crescendo
of herring-bones and the lighthouse slowly crumbled.

My First Lobster

My lover brought me a lobster
fresh from the Pentland Firth.
My lover wove the creel, steered the boat,
laid the trap, hauled the rope,
boiled the catch.

The lobster was beautiful,
Pink naked in newspaper.
My lover said, the best is in the tail.
I tore the claws and knuckles, butter sticky,
sucking, licking, probing, splitting,
searching soft white meat.

Afterwards,
shell broken, belly filled with seawater
I dreamed of the ocean floor
and my lover waiting.

SERENADE

Her feet were jelly fish stranded in a rock pool
or filo pastry left in the rain
and her toes were marbles lost under the sofa.
And her ankles were secret trapdoors
and her legs were ships lost in the Haar
and her thighs were a terrorist ambush.
Her crotch was a picnic under a shady tree
or a foreign film with subtitles
and her vagina was a waiting room with velvet sofas.
Her stomach was a piano keyboard
or a bottled gas cooker
and her waist was Fingal's Cave
and her ribs were hieroglyphs found at Skara Brae
and her buttocks were exclamation marks!!
Her breasts were cumulus clouds at sunset
or thermonuclear weapons
or lamps in a distant window.
The crooks of her elbows were pistachios
and her arms were War and Peace
or bulldozers on a building site
and her hands were Olympians.
Her spine was a rope bridge over a canyon
or an Aeolian harp
and her shoulders were white whales.
Her neck was a seagull diving
and her chin was King Canute
and her cheeks were beech leaves used as bookmarks
and her skin was Flamenco.
The tips of her ears were whipped cream
and her teeth were a cryptic puzzle
or the standing stones at Callanich.
Her eyes were a film by David Cronenberg
or Mississippi Mud Pie in a late-night café.
And her eyebrows were squeezed tubes of tooth paste
and her nose was a wind turbine on a Scottish hill
and her mouth was a furnace manufacturing steel rods
or a jewellery box lined with jade.
And her hair was the wings of a gypsy moth
or frosted willow branches
or a moonlit path
to an unknown destination.

FORGETTING MOZART

We met the second
time in the old scarlet fever hospital.
You were pale as sea-pebbles.
We followed the beat of Arabian
drums down secret passages,
footsteps echoing on linoleum.
Rain pelted
prestissimo at the skylight.

I put Mozart on ice, played Sad
Eyed Lady of the Lowlands for you,
arpeggio style. *Don't need melody* you said,
hunched in the shadows with your heroin
cheekbones and roll-ups.
You turned the lights down on your way out,
left me smeared across the ivory.
Don't need complicated, you said.

So I learned simple chords, A major, E minor,
two of us on the piano stool, free style.
Not looking for a solo but looking
for adagio down the motorway
shooting out the window with my Lomo.
I was looking for a car crash.
I was looking for a mindless.
Don't need money, as you took my last fiver.

We met the last time as the sun
fell into the lake and a murder
of crows ripped from the birch.
In the twilight everything
was almost alright, *alright?*
There was a moment when I saw a new
moon over your shoulder, a moment
when we almost touched.

UNBOUND

One day you'll write about us,
you said on your last visit.
A starry love story, a film…
Betty Blue meets Quadrophenia,
you said. I said,
but how will it end?
As I left you at Central Station
you said, *I'm missing you already.*
I said, *never,* remembering silence
as we drove deep through Kielder forest.

There's a bond between us
that can't be broken,
you wrote in your last letter.
Blood, sex, magic
you said. I said,
I'm sick of bleeding
and magic's not real
and there's more to life than fucking.
I want to be cherished.
You said, *that's cloying.*

Sometimes, naked on star-less nights
I Google your name and wait.

The A to Z of Love

Absence is the heart of Love a brutal
Board game for two or more
Capricious players intent on self
Delusion a power struggle not
Enlightenment or hope for the spiritual
Frisson of two strangers touching skin
Gestures an attempt at unexpected soul
Happiness is a voidable experiment not
Intended to last more than ninety nine
Joyful but repetitive days when ruinous
Keepsakes fall like autumn rain before
Love breakfasts lessen to burnt toast
Marmite with cold coffee because
No-one notices cloud formations or
Opens their eyes to truly see another
Person is not the perfect answer to every
Question but more questions that require
Rumination and lead to rheumatism and
Slavery but do not give up hope bitter
Times do not last and love is not worthless
Undressing in the dark nor a virtuous
Virus causing fever flush and accelerated
Weeping at weekends instead
Xpect expectations to be compromised
You will not be satisfied unless you are a
Zealot intent on annihilation.

OLD FLAME

so good to see you
smoke-eyed stranger in the night
with blood on your teeth

when you spark that talk
sly fruit bloom on sullen trees
starlings fall like snow

I remember you
burning sweet Ballachulish
heather by the loch

in a hotel room
shadowed by the Three Sisters
and scented orange

we hoped our extinct
volcano might come to life
in that flash of light

Through the Cracks of Winter

we camped in the Black Mountains
and you thought you saw a wolf. I was a stain
in the shadow of a great cliff of sturdy construction
with a hinged lid. The shoe-box of Hiroshima,
can we forget that flash? How did God shine
the light in the passing space, not minding
as lemmings dived? She had Her own intentions.

I let night over my head like cling film
on a frozen turkey, smoothing the bitter lines.
Then you looked up and described a dream,
the sun scrambled on New Year's Day. Your words
consumed another, one for every minute.
At midnight you stood beneath the pines singing
Jerusalem. I broke free and soared
in the middle of it all, crazy laughing
as the reservoir rotted red as sunset. I was the one
who once loved you, with your yes, yes, yes until
the world shouted no, do not drive or use machines.

You were the watchman of my panopticon.
I was a clock ticking.

GIFTS

The first spilled secrets in filthy school loos.
The second gave ginger cut to the chase.
The third made love, death and crime on Ward 5.
The fourth shared The Sound of Silence.
The fifth fell into a snow drift.
The sixth surrendered beautiful on the banks of the Tyne.
The seventh gave a wedding ring and split lip.
The eighth made excellent chicken soup.
The ninth gave gin massage on hot lawns.
The tenth offered midnight lifts to therapy and falling stars.
The eleventh staged punctures in motorway service stations.
The twelfth gave tarot card readings.
The thirteenth banned the Bomb and taught self-defence
with a spanner, sickle and hammer.
He slept with his socks on.
The fifteenth performed impressions of Richard Gere.
The sixteenth gave empty, like Dire Straits.
The seventeenth cracked my zoom lens.
The nineteen rowed my boat to the island of woolly mammoths.
The twenty second shared Victoria Sandwich and arson.
The twenty eighth gave life drawing. He jumped off the High Level Bridge.
The thirty sixth sent crocodiles under my floor.
The one after him played a mean pianissimo and made the top forty.
The last one believed in the theory of reincarnation.

SONG

She who is composition in blue and orange.
She who is ice water tumbling on rocks.
She who is top of the tower.
She who is willow bending in the wind.
She who is Chopin Nocturne 72.
She who is meeting the devil at the crossroads.
She who is strawberry wine with a dash of cyanide.
She who is white wolf hunting by moonlight.
She who is neon or xenon or argon or helium, balloons floating.
She who has been crash tested in extreme situations.
She who has no centre of gravity.
She who will leave dirt tracks all over your fat face.
She who has small sharp white teeth.
She who has sensational performance.
She who has eye of the kestrel.
She who is splendid in solitude.
She who is child of Kali.
She who is revolving door.
She who is crack in the plaster.
She who is razor's edge.
She who is smell of hot tarmac.
She who is cripple bitch.
She who is me.

PLASTICINE

You are nothing but a clatter of bones in a dressing gown
coughing up phlegm over our breakfast table.
You are nothing but a slither of liver, lungs, kidneys, brain,
faithless heart pumping white crimson around and around.
You are nothing but a hundred billion neurons firing arrow
thoughts about yourself into a mist of grey.
You stab the butter knife in the marmalade.
I want to stab it in your eye, see your ego bleed out.

Suddenly you look at me and describe a dream
you had about building a house from Plasticine.
As you turn your face and smile, morning sunbeams
blaze just below the curve of your cheek
bone, the place I kiss before we sleep
cool and sharp as an underground stream.

THE CROSSING

Spheres of eau de nil slip through, careless.
The island glimmers like crushed glass.

She doesn't look up when I speak
the sound of silence spiked with roses.

She is wearing a wolf jacket, face tilted
and edged with gold. A fandango is a gift

not for everywoman, she was someone
ten minutes before and her own name

centre stage. Now she prays as the invisible
life of the sea spills skywards. Pink naked

in newspapers, dislocation strikes a pose.
She turns. No place for strangers they say.

The first time is the hardest and she twists
for her dreams. I want to laugh until

I see rain pelting cheekbones and roll-ups.
Where was my power over water?

Wait for Me

your roses bloom
in winter
                        turn to rust
your companion
is black magic
                        a willow tree
your sea sparks
treasure at twilight
                        galvanised
your wind tastes
of lavender
                        blows crushed glass
your watermelons
smell of sunrise
                        shrivel like mice
your cheeks are plump
as summer
                        sweet opium
your sins
are forgiven
                        lie underground
your sons sprout
high as fountains
                        drowned before birth
your neighbours
sweep away demons
                        pass me in the street
your cupboards
hold dusty memories
                        crammed with lace
your blue walls
fade to newspaper
                        a crystal ball
you leave
doors open
                        and I will come

THE OTHER SIDE

Somewhere in the Hambleton Hills
I took a right turn down a track not
on any map and edgy with yesterday.

Like Alice I plunged down a tunnel
of yellow gorse, silver birch and rocks
that had danced in the Book of Genesis.

A large pink dog, the sort that calls
a spade a spade was waiting by a stream
where the track vanished in a tangle

of weeping willows and a warning sign
Check depth before entering. Deep water
and shadows beckoned. The dog wagged

his tail in approval and I saw beyond
the ford; a fertile valley and sheep
like ballerinas in tutus and a rainbow

house on a hill in a dazzle of sublime
clouds. I saw a smiling face and a hand
waving, an orchard and a rose garden.

I smelled strawberries, fresh bread
and wood smoke. The whispers of leaves
and birdsong drifted on the breeze.

The dog waited, his eyes wary as hope
while I considered the darkness
of the crossing and judged it too deep.

A Different Place

Far, far better than we, a huddle
of caterpillars in the shape of a heart
emerges from beneath the tree roots.

When the brick walls fall to ground
I give them their marching orders. Time
is short if you have imperial longings.

A cloud of soil settles at my feet, falling
bodies. I never had a head for heights.
Possession is a never-ending

source of magic. Body and flame
find their significance. Fingernails, skin,
hair, teeth, white fingers edging

the fields with hope. I used to love
like that, without concealment, grabbing
the light of her with no distance between.

Now is a different place entirely. The gravel
road goes ever on and on to the wicked
songs of the north. The pale April

sun looks down these lines of envious hills.
We travel great distances in search
of a mate and return when we are worn.

I feel suddenly at home and inhale
all that remains; a swathe of blue, eleven
apple trees and a citadel of painted ladies.

BLUE

I am one speck of dust passing through.
I am silk thread unraveling
the caterpillar inside her cocoon.

I am the blood of winter
sun beyond the horizon
and I float a murmur of starlings.

I brood a melancholy song
whispering blue into the wind.
I glide the last seeds from the sycamore.

I hunt the moon with moth-silver wings
and streak midnight skies with electricity.
I skim my love with words touching skin.

I breathe one thought between me and you.
I am one speck of dust passing through.

ABOUT THE AUTHOR

Lydia Popowich was born in Yorkshire to parents of Ukrainian origin who arrived in Britain as war refugees in 1947. Her maternal grandfather was a writer and political dissident in the former Soviet Union and he was one of Lydia's main influences.

After teacher training, a politics degree, various jobs and marriage she went on to study visual art in Newcastle upon Tyne during the nineties where she specialised in photography. For many years she worked as a community artist and her artwork was widely exhibited. She was a Green Party activist, a founding member of Northern Disability Arts Forum and a campaigner for disability rights.

In 2005 Lydia moved to the Far North of Scotland. Her writing has appeared in anthologies and literary journals including Magma, Ambit, Under the Radar and Northwords Now. Her first poetry pamphlet, The Jellyfish Society was published in 2016 by Paper Swans Press. Lydia is the editor of The Haar creative arts e-zine and author of The Purple Hermit blog.

.

Printed in Great Britain
by Amazon